TONBRIDGE SCHOOL LIBRARY

Remember to check your books out on the computer.
Stamp this label with the date for return.

– ROLLING STACK –

Mrs Power Looks Over the Bay

FERGUS ALLEN

faber and faber

First published in 1999
by Faber and Faber Limited
3 Queen Square London WC1N 3AU

Photoset by Wilmaset Ltd, Wirral
Printed in England by MPG Books Limited,
Victoria Square, Bodmin, Cornwall

© Fergus Allen, 1999

Fergus Allen is hereby identified as author of this
work in accordance with Section 77 of the Copyright,
Designs and Patents Act 1988

A CIP record for this book
is available from the British Library

ISBN 0-571-20029-X

10 9 8 7 6 5 4 3 2 1

for Joan

Acknowledgements

My thanks are due to the editors of the following
magazines, in which a number of these poems, or versions
of them, first appeared: *Acumen*, *London Magazine*, *Metre*,
P.N. Review, *Poetry Ireland Review*, *Poetry London
Newsletter*, *Poetry Review*, *The Recorder* (NY),
Thumbscrew and *Times Literary Supplement*.

Versions of 'The Lifeboat' and 'East Cliff, West Bay' first
appeared in *West Bay* (The Rocket Press, 1997).

'Glenasmole' was included in *Or Volge L'Anno – At the
Year's Turning*, an anthology edited by Marco Sonzogni
and sponsored by the Italian Cultural Institute in Dublin to
mark the bicentenary of the birth of Giacomo Leopardi.

Contents

Mrs Power Looks Over the Bay

To Be Read Before Being Born

No time is allowed for practice or rehearsal,
There are no retakes and there isn't a prompter.
There's only moving water, dimpled by turbulence –
And no clambering out on to the bank
To think things over, as there is no bank.

Two-Day-Old Grandchild

FOR JOSEPH DOHERTY

The sun heaves up out of the sea,
Blinks and props himself on his elbow:
'I asked you to call me at six,

'So much has to be done by noon,
The electorate to be wooed,
A frog to be found and kissed.

'From the castle I'm going to be king of
The estate must be overseen
By my unmeetable eye.'

Hide yourself from this workaholic
Or give the appearance of sleep,
With your dishy little lips ajar

To ward off fate, and miniature hands
Like those of a lemur expelled
From blood-hot Malagasy darkness.

The world will be with you soon enough,
The Palace Pier will say 'Hullo dearie'
And show you her barnacled legs,

Wavelets will fawn on you like spaniels
And the voluptuous Pavilion
Will call out to you in her sleep.

But now you must come to terms with gravity
And the air that insists on filling
Your spotless lungs and fans your skin,

And also with the puzzling images
On your retina and the incessant
Murmurs of approbation.

A Young Protestant Lady

As Mrs McGraw, our cook, had sent word
That she was laid up in bed with a bad leg,
And May, who comes to skivvy in the mornings,
Was going round groaning about her monthlies,
I said I'd skim the cream before it turned.

It was cool down in the dairy, with muslin
Pinned across the lights, greenish at ground level,
For keeping out bluebottles and dung flies.
The cream clung to the skimmer like the crew
Of the *Medusa* to their slippery raft,

Upstairs father sailed through yesterday's paper
And I thought about last year in the dairy
When Adam came, and I was walking slowly
Round the table with its big pans of milk.
You could hear my skirts and underthings rustle

And I knew for sure he wanted to kiss me.
But nothing happened. We just tasted the cream
As if it were uisce beatha (which it could have been),
And he went off to his dogs, always his dogs,
Dribbling, and rolling their bootlicker's eyes.

Dogs' looks are no threat to a man's self-esteem –
Something all the Irish boys seem to fret about.
Their manliness seems to be so precious
You'd think it had been lifted out of a lake
By an arm wrapped in a length of white samite.

6

Dinner-time wasn't as glum as it can be
And when father had had his glass of stout
He told us how Sir Walter Scott was dead,
And the price of corn, and how the new railways
Would creep down from Dublin like hairy mollies.

Mama sat through this with the same half-smile
She always wears at meal-times, like a lighthouse
Whose lamp is turned off in the hours of daylight.
Afternoons she escapes into her watercolours,
An album of wild flowers picked in the paddock.

Sempervirens, she whispers to herself,
Sucking her paint-brush, mixing the green bice
To lay in tearfuls on the Whatman paper,
Palustris, magic of Linnæan Latin,
Better than alkanet and those other names.

Killing or breeding is what goes on elsewhere,
Illusions of creation and scorched earth –
But there, I'm talking like one of those Buddhists,
Not a believer in the risen Christ.
Over in Ross Uncle John is a banker,

He lends other people's money to third parties,
Seeming to do quite nicely. And at home,
Multiplying faster than yeast in a vat,
My blue-eyed cousins overflow his house.
They remind me of plumbago in July.

Far-sighted father gave me this plain gold ring
(The only one I think I'll ever get),
Which some remote descendant I can't imagine
May wear on his little finger when I'm dead
And mention in a poem, and think of me.

Latent Heat

In the Moravian cemetery, Whitechurch,
the dead are buried upright, on their feet
under uniform capstones, his or hers,
ready for the last trump and Resurrection;

and flecked by the elm-light of late July
the girl from 2A, for whom I've been a cypher,
brushes against me, bare arm against bare shoulder,
her skin milky cool and easily dimpled.

Knowing there is no such thing as an accident,
this comes as big news to an only child.
The dust-devil of sensation takes over,
supervised by Morgan le Fay or some such.

Years on, when I check in to adolescence,
the whole caravanserai will be shaking
to music, while behind a rusted gate
the dead Moravians still stand and wait.

Parental Guidance

Nobody warned me that life would contain
Swearing and scenes of violence and nudity.
There may have been references to the poor
And of course there were children without shoes
Around Gardiner Street and Mountjoy Square;
There was also a time called the Great War,
Whose after-effects could be seen on crutches;
And sometimes the Inquisition was mentioned,
As was the influenza epidemic,
In which my Uncle Reginald had died.

But none of this fitted in with the noises
I could hear in that hotel in Duncannon,
Audible through the lath-and-plaster wall,
The crying, the thumps, the half-suppressed squeals.
Who could be hurting whom? And yet at breakfast,
Around the stiff antarctic table-cloth,
Moustached Mr Ganly in his striped shirt
Was genial over the porridge and haddock,
And Mrs G spoke mildly of the weather
As she brushed crumbs off her flowery blouse.

I can see you know what I have in mind.
Today, however, we shall cross the estuary
In a pale-blue clinker-built boat and fish
For whatever's there, probably mackerel.
Bags I not pull the hooks from the fishes' mouths
Or do what I have seen them do to eels.

(I'd thought that crab on the quayside was dead,
But a claw flexed and a leg stirred when I looked
And he was watching me through small black eyes.
I do not want a half-dead crab for supper.)

When I shook my head at the tramp, his words
Were tangled up by drink and broken teeth,
But I could tell his wishes were malign.
His threats trailed after me all the way home,
Lingering for days just outside the gate.
And at school, over empty playing-fields,
The autumn's starlings arrived on manoeuvres
While the sixth form stripped for the showers, ivory
Bodies steaming and singing in the stalls,
Proud of their genitals and broken voices.

Funny if it were otherwise, I think,
Example being the larger part of learning.
But there's always the unheroic option
Of watching from a locked and darkened car
As the possessed, beside themselves, take over
All that I tell myself I do not want
(Finding reassurance in the sour grapes).
And later on, within a sterile room,
I could enclose my hands in rubber gloves
And draft a protocol of separation.

In the Gaeltacht

Over the half-door, the new sun picking out
The night's snowfall up on the Knockmealdowns
And always a cormorant, with a low profile
   Taking its course to Helvick Head.

Packed off there to learn from the native speakers,
I had my first taste of Player's Navy Cut
And studied the advice and observations
   Scribbled obliquely on the walls

Of the not insalubrious earth closet.
Written in English, these were not beyond me.
And each Saturday, if the rain kept off,
   There was a ceilidhe at the cross-roads.

The dance floor was small, springy as willow,
The player squeezed and fingered his accordion
And we made the rounds of 'The Walls of Limerick'.
   Known to all as 'Falla Luimnigh'.

I was too young for stout and beneath the notice
Of the girls who stood waiting to be asked.
(Anyway I believed myself in love
   With some Beatrice back at school.)

But everyone smiled, and their hands and lips
Guided me through the patterns like a fugitive
Being passed from one safe house to the next.
   Perhaps I was a changeling child.

So the shoes rattled on the boards, and heads
Bobbed up and down against the evening sky,
Balloons of thoughts, unreadable to me,
   Rising into the pink light of sunset.

I dwelt with Bean uí Skuce, under whose roof
I failed to grow proficient in the medium,
But learned to smoke a fag from end to end
   With the aid of a household pin.

Kathleen Mavourneen in Omagh

The day the harp exploded on her knee –
That was when deconstruction came of age
And meaning smothered in the shit of rage.
They knew the cameras would race to see
Splashes of blood, a future amputee,
Parents despairing in an empty cage.
Nothing was now too awful for the stage,
The old-time censor was a refugee.

Motive had as much meaning as a fart,
Pain was what mattered, what was understood,
Watching its vivid symptoms gave them joy.
The message flew directly to the heart –
This was their world, the contrary of good,
And you were one of those the gods destroy.

Odyssey

That country might have had much to show me,
but I as usual had to catch
the next train or the first flight or ferry
into someone or other's good books.

I looked back at the betel palms, waving
over the crowded, commercial town
and recognized the familiar twinges
of rapport no sooner made than broken.

Perhaps not made at all. Spun from sugar
and the smell of wood smoke and the chit-chat
of women washing clothes by the river,
witnessed by me, smiling with my camera.

I know I shall be missing the best—
the awards, the love affair, the orgy—
but new landfalls may offer new treats
(for which I must load another film),

unless of course I'm called away again—
which, as I know in my heart, I shall be—
to some desk or bedside or tribunal
and brought to account for falling short.

More painful are Dalkey and Killiney,
the same old slate-grey against grey clouds,
wrapped up in their own affairs and facing me
with neither welcome nor curiosity.

In the Airport Coach

Something goes on behind her head,
Small naked animals at work,
No, it's her hand, a pair of hands,
Action-packed self-reliant fingers
That comb out and divide her hair,
Shiny, after-shampooing hair,
Into equal tresses for braiding –
And all the time her eyes take in
The passing churches, crucifixions,
Pale pietàs and dolours of Phibsborough,
From which the dew has dried,
And the façades of licensed premises
With their marbling and secrecy.

No-nonsense digits (wedding-ring crowding
The sapphire and diamond three-stone)
Plait fast and sure, knowing their business,
Pass strand over strand without a glance
At third parties or books of rules.
Loose ends secured, the queues are coiled,
Lifted up, back – the index pushing,
Prodding and testing – interwoven,
While motherly words are delivered
To a girl-child who wriggles, points
And teases her with questions.

Santry, and the clamour of aircraft
Brings hairdressing to a head.
Now pins: thumb and forefinger poised
(They must have eyes as well as strength)
To skewer down the twisted bun
Quickly, without irresolution.
Remind me, tell me again what else
The hand that rocks the cradle does.

Mrs Power Looks Over the Bay

Spring is upon us again and the rivers
are up to their eyes in finding themselves an ocean.
Just now there's brightness on the coast opposite,
but those dishevelled clouds will soon come crowding in
when they've made their seasonal getaway
from Iceland or thereabouts.

Out of the house, please, and down to the shop
where yesterday's order is mouldering in its carton –
mixed groceries that seem proud to be foreign.
And bring the cattle back from the strand
before the almanac catches up with them
and you and the rest of us.

O'Reilly's yard-dogs come from a brood of heathens,
snarling and slavering, like all black-and-tans.
I and your father modelled them in candlegrease
and stuck poisoned bodkins into their bellies,
but of course they're immune to that kind of stunt.
Some kind of trap would do better.

Those holier-than-thou mountains have plenty to hide,
they never refer to the past, no kidding,
but they take it out of the broken-winded Volvo
when we have a fancy to go on a visit.
Like-minded people put fairings in the window
and wagers on dark horses.

On sunny days the sea lies out there like armour
on a breathing zombie, one of the undead
we saw on last Saturday's television,
but, as Mikey said, the smell of burning tyres
drifting up from the childrens' playground
takes the magic out of it.

My brother Liam used to practise his semaphore
with the rest of the team above on the cliff-top,
close to the landmark we called the Metal Man.
But that's a while ago, long before the coastguards
got electricity. Anyway Willy is dead
and has been twenty years.

If there's still a lookout, it's full of broken glass
and sprayed comments on the local talent.
These days the fish have moved offshore or been taken
in their youth by Spanish trawlers or the French,
and the tankers on the horizon are too grand
to give you the time of day.

'Halcyon' was an adjective we learned at school,
and on that sort of morning, when the water's flat
from here to South America and the gulls have hushed,
a seal may push its head up out of the water
and take its bearings like a wartime U-boat
en route for the sea-roads,

or stay there without moving, staring in disbelief
at the farm and its outhouses and goings-on,
like a visitor to a zoo, rapt in the life
of some alien and inferior species,
and thinking with some truth that the lot of us
are as plain as turnips,

then lower her brimming eyes and sink
with barely a ripple into the past.
I'd swear I'd seen a head like that on the drummer
of a show band that came down here for a wedding
last Easter and played till all hours in a pink marquee —
sleek, with a titchy moustache.

If you've done your homework give your daddy a hand
with the tractor that seems to be giving birth
and before the rain comes driving through the wall
to spoil the fodder. Oh I've come a long way
with your father since our skins first touched
like fruit in a bowl.

I've told you how he came over by country bus,
ready to see off those stagy jackdaws
who had shouldered their way into the back garden,
loosening the guns in their holsters and not caring
about the sea mist that blew across and wetted
their round grey heads.

And about the boat that was dragged up on the shingle,
which he hired to go crabbing just off the point,
and how we were carried out to sea by the rip
after we'd lost the two oars through our carrying-on.
But we wound the clocks on Sunday nights before exposing
our pearl-buttoned fantasies.

Of course you and your friends don't know you're born,
what with modern medicine and your screens lit up
all the day and night with coloured promises.
Aren't you the lucky ones? Not so long ago,
as your grandmother said, it wasn't just the poor
that died of consumption.

The Autobiography of a Leman

I was born at the foot of a hill
Where water welled up out of the limestone
And the brambles that gathered around
Had rags and prayers tied to their stems.
My growing-up was done among shades
While my parents stood with their ears cocked,
Listening to noises from the past
And what they feared might be the screams
Of the unattended on the battlefield.

In the years of gathering momentum,
When I was magnifying myself
And repeatedly changing my skin,
All the elms along the drive were felled
And their timber stolen to make coffins.
A forester with pox was arrested,
But (surprise!) the charges did not stick.
By the time I was ready for bravery
The earth's face had been shaved and tarred.

The Great Northern Hotel set the tone
For pleasures that trickled down like linctus,
Soothing the itches of eschatology.
The ceiling was so high, cirro-stratus,
Concealing our actions from the sun,
And breakfast came on a tray, the maid
Discreet, and we topped the eggs and dipped
Our soldiers into the runny yellow.
But plain sailing all the way it wasn't.

Casanova's not even my middle name.
A feather mattress (you've never tried one?)
Is more maternal than seductive,
And movements in an adjoining room,
The proximity of ears and tell-tales,
Halt the train a long way down the track,
Which makes for an anti-climax. Still,
As a father figure might have said,
One can but try. And at least it's cosy.

When I went off with somebody serious
(Yes, yes, I know there were others later)
And we kissed in the Silvermine Mountains,
The light of day was barred from the cottage
By our mirrors of infatuation
And money minded its own business.
The faithful trannie sang along with us
As we filled the kettle at the spring,
Me running my finger up her thigh.

Then there were the years among the oranges.
Being kept was not something that bothered me,
I could pull my weight, put out the bin
On Thursday evenings, switch on the miniature
Fountain to freshen the goldfish pond
And give as good as I got in love
(Not forgetting the sauces and condiments).
Mosquitoes cruised around in the bedroom,
The huerta's frogs carried on all night.

But home's in the vale, the lee of Djouce,
Where the rain-shadow hides our misdoings
(Though I would never have called them that)
And the late bus brings us back from Roundwood
And *pintade en daube* at the Silver Trout
To aspirations under the duvet.
If it wasn't for the jackdaws clamouring
For food after the eight o'clock news,
I think we mightn't get up at all.

But all that's in the historic present.
Reality, here and now, is different:
East wind, and the larches can no longer
Get their corky twigs around the syllables
Of my vanishing name; gusts are tugging
At the revers of my buttonless raincoat,
Which I ineffectually clutch
With fingers steadily growing numb
As the air turns colder towards sunset.

The Outing

By the time we had all got off the barge
It was time for the picnic – thick ham sandwiches,
With an acid drink of partly dissolved
Lemonade crystals in enamel mugs
And the choice of an apple or banana.
Then it was walks – up the riverine cliff
To the joylessness of a Norman keep,
A set left over from some looter's tragedy,
Actors' names forgotten, the programme lost;
Or brushing through the meadowsweet and rushes
With a following of flies, to the privacy
Of a hazel thicket where the salmon leapt
In its wisdom and where I might be cheered
By your blood-hot fingers and chilly thighs.

Fire

A fairly good summer in Balrothery
Had left things dry, the carline thistle-heads
Covered with long-bodied rufous beetles,
Cow-pats caked on the uneven pasture
And dung-flies alighting on my skin
With the stealth of Blackshirt at a door.

We walked up Tymon Lane towards Greenhills,
Me holding my father's hand, my lassitude
Well to the fore as always, while buses
Bound for Tallaght grumbled past behind us
(Or it might have been the ancient steam-tram,
Heading for Blessington and the golden west).

That day the west was a slatey cloudbank –
But why did I hear a cyclone roar
Through invisible trees, and the crash
Of branches falling? Over a rise,
Through gaps in a blackthorn hedge, we saw
Suddenly a building full of flame,

A timber barn, weatherproofed with pitch,
Blazing from end to end and top to bottom.
It filled the world with orange light, raging
At the little figures that ran around
And waved their hands helplessly in front of it.
It called out, and not only to sinners.

That was my meeting with the big world,
A world where nothing was to be trusted.
Even now, waking on a bright morning,
When the sun warms the blind and the singleton
Peacock cries out for a mate, I know
What hangs precariously over my head.

Child Father to Man

The water-coloured hills say nothing
And I am saying nothing back.
They stand for scratches and fatigue
In the there and then, quite unlike
The soothing mother's milk they promised.

Here and now, in an undrained grazing,
Cinnabar moths are sussing out
The yellow nurseries of ragwort;
I pause, damp-footed among horsetails,
As purposeless as an appendix.

Then peering through a hawthorn hedge
I see my past self in a field,
An undersized dissembling boy.
'So interested in insects', they said,
'But tiring quickly after lunch.'

Aged eleven, in the treble register,
I was not at a loss for words;
Always discontented, of course,
And wanting to be somewhere else –
A right little pain in the neck.

But quick enough to oil the wheels
When my comforts were under threat,
When venerable locomotives
With leaking glands got steamed up
In rusty Victorian sheds.

That field held little except vacation
From encouragement and loving care.
As a tortoiseshell paused to probe
Some boring flower, I lifted my eyes
To Mount Venus and the Hell Fire Club.

A Wet Afternoon

A page of narrative and, verso,
the illustration of Sir Bors
standing there dismounted in his hauberk,
sword point-downward among the weeds.
Helmet and beaver laid aside
he looks over the reader's shoulder,
gaze pensive and *fin de siècle*.
A housefly walks across the book,
flitting to the rim of my teacup
to wash its hands of my future.

Where has the wind wandered away to?
Rain glides like glycerine from laurels
on to last year's leathery leaves.
And a hairy comet hangs fire
over a child's idea of willows,
witnessed by an eye-rolling Saxon
who holds out his ploughman's hands
for an intercession of saints.
Elsewhere I can hear bogies squealing
as the trams turn into their stables.

Thinly clad for a German January,
the king's daughter rides on her plough-wheel
over the twice-three cutting swords
to free the prince, moustache and all,
from his iron stove in the forest.
She will partake of his inheritance,
her green sickness a thing of the past,

while we cast lots and share our ennui,
waiting for a break in the clouds
and a walk with our peccadillos.

Rashly launched, my aeroplane flew
across the ten-foot limestone wall
into the stillness of the Carmelites.
I have mislaid my ball in the knotweed
and my resolve among the currants,
where the doctor's daughter undid me.
Now, through the wet window, I watch
the wine-stains of October spread
like guilt over the hanging woods.
They might be spillage from a grail

or tell-tales on a battlefield –
like those we have engravings of.
But killing time is today's programme,
holding my breath or counting heart-beats
or scrutinizing a drop of blood
under the birthday-present microscope
and failing to make out the corpuscles,
or tutoring our mynah bird
in mimicry, to cheer me up
with wanted words, spoken sincerely.

Waltzing with Veronica

As a diminutive boy I had to dance backwards,
While my adolescent partner steered the two of us
Round and round the Saturday-evening dance-floor.

Not very macho, perhaps, but hints of bliss
Came when I sensed her animal vigour and rested
My small head between her jersey-covered breasts.

'Roses from the South' left me giddy and speechless –
And sad, when Miss Maloney thumped the last chord
And the coloured lights went out in all our heads.

Palmerston Park

As it comes back to me, the fountain
Had the form of an upturned fir-cone,
The scales gaping, the seed expelled.
Children ran around it and screamed,
But it had never been known to play –
Or not since the Diamond Jubilee.
It stood dead centre in the pond
And there was always a little water
Dribbling out of its rusty holes.
This was colonialism in decay.

Not that we knew it. Michael Collins
Was only a few years dead
And ourselves a few years alive.
Mr Brady was our tyrant;
He raged out of the gardeners' lair,
Shouting about corporation by-laws.
In Bath chairs beside his barbered lawn
And beds of geranium and alyssum
Sat one or other of the 'shell-shocked' men
Whose hands lay trembling on their knees.

With their weak eyes and waxy faces
They made us shy, we wished them elsewhere.
What was all this about a war?
A story from the olden days.
But beyond the Corsican pines
A perfect ball flew upwards, paused
Against the summer blue and fell

Down to the voices of a pack
Unworried by transubstantiation
Or prohibitory signs.

Some drank out of an iron cup
That was chained to the iron pillar,
While others held their hollowed hands
Under the gush from a lion's mouth.
The latter were mothers' boys,
Conscious of national anthems,
Flags and contagion. But reports
Of slap-bangs and percussion caps
Were not enough to undermine
A passing seagull's equipoise.

There are snakes below the gutter,
Said my friend Desmond, crossing his heart.
He pointed to a hard-faced house
That held up its turret as a threat
Among monkey puzzles and calp.
A madman lives there, he insisted,
Listen and you can hear him roar.
But when the wind dropped all I heard
Was a protestant dog and trickling
Of rain-water into a shore.

Palmerston, Kenilworth and Grosvenor –
All those taken-for-granted names.
Was this an Indian cantonment,
Lee Enfields stacked and at the ready?
Five, and the bell for closing time
Rang like an untrue mawkish symbol.
At nine tomorrow Mr Brady,
After a drag, would grasp his stick
And ready himself to counter
The rising generation's crime.

The Ferry

It was more of a whaler than a ferry,
Wide and heavily built, with such high gunwales
I'm sure you could have drifted out to sea in it
And come to no harm from waves or God.
The two gruff ferrymen were built to match,
Each with an oar a good fifteen foot long.

When the tide was running out they aimed
Obliquely up-river to the grain silos,
But on the flood they pointed the bows
Nearly east, more or less towards Faithlegg.
Either way they always managed to land us
By the concrete steps, slippery with silt.

It was a penny for a ten-minute crossing —
A hard pull on a diet of fried bread.
If either were taken bad we could be swept
On to the piers of the bridge a mile up
Or carried off seawards in the rain
And whirled round in the eddies off Cheek Point.

They rowed the twelve of us across to Christendom,
Against whom we played cricket once a year.
Christendom were older but less well coached.
It was there I saw the man with a rook rifle,
Whose oily gleam and undecorated stock
Showed it to be a serious firearm.

As we passed him by with our cricket-bags
He summed us up with a look, and taking
A copying pencil from behind his ear
Scribbled something on the back of a matchbox.
With his olive face and derisive smile
He was the kind of man some women like.

Minutes later we heard a shot and, turning,
Saw black feathers falling out of a tree.
Then Saturday silence and the crunch
Of cricketing boots on the limestone dust.
Near the end of that match I took a wicket
When I tried out my unreliable leg break.

Going back to school we passed Clover Meats
And its sausage factory, running with blood;
Then the ferry again, before a storm
Wetted us through and had us dreaming forward
To the baths and Lifebuoy soap and, later,
The calm white coverlets of the dormitory.

The Visitant

They were shocked to see me, or so it looked,
When I dropped into the year 1860.
Quite amazing was the physical detail,
More than I thought I could have dreamt up, real,

Quite unstagy, just the John Trot of living,
Serges dusty, even traces of food
On their lapels and bibs (the soaps were harsh
And dry-cleaning a brainwave of the future).

There was a cousin, many times removed,
Of whom I had seen a Lafayette photograph,
And my grandmother (née Spinks), just a child –
Not marionettes acting on my dictates,

But all self-willed and lively, full of bustle,
And now aghast in the hall, though indifferent
To who I was or where I might have come from
(That of course is something I've grown well used to).

Through the blisters of damp on Nile-green walls
I could just make out fasces and crossed axes –
A poorly drawn and touching attempt at grandeur –
And the black-and-white floor showed muddy bootprints.

I complimented my cousin by marriage
On her gathered dress – in poplin or bombazine,
Dark grey shot with violet – and it seemed
A half smile stole across her knobbly features

As though she'd heard me. 'Can't you see it, James?'
She cried out loudly in a country accent
To a pompous-looking beard, who was wool-gathering
In a frock coat (it must have been a Sunday).

But by then I was fading like a sunrise.
From rough grass in the garden I looked back
To see the said James behind a window,
Still bemused among his female manipulators,

And, on the sill, colourful souvenirs
That collectors of the future would bid for.
Beyond the hedge, between the banks of butterbur,
The railway to Rosslare stretched out expectantly,

Though most of the time it was left to rust.
Just twice a day – weekdays, morning and evening –
A train would rumble past, pale faces staring
From the third class at pastures full of thistle.

Over the water is where they were bound for,
This way and that, into a past or future,
On tracks spiked to creosoted sleepers
Above which I was hovering like a kestrel.

Fishers of Fish

Spinning for mackerel off Ballycotton
(or it may have been hake, hake was what we caught)
with a north wind putting a chill in the air,
the old-fashioned petrol engine packed up
and we drifted away downwind for miles,
the shore diminishing to a foreign hairline,
while Chris and Evelyn, making the best of it,
rubbed their fingers for warmth and fixed their smiles.

As for me, with my B+ in Geography,
I could picture us out of sight and mind,
driven tangentially past Finisterre
to fetch up finally at Gran Canary
where, seeing our stiffened limbs and pecked-at eyes,
fishermen's mothers would cross themselves and pray.
Our small coffins shipped home with the bananas
would be unloaded under watery skies.

But Terry, priming the motor yet again,
brought it to life and us out of our daydreams.
Turning into the wind we all lit up,
sheltering our matches under the cowl,
and there was fresh salt on our lips and teeth
as we threw lines into the turbulent wake
and waited. Minutes later we hauled them in
with creatures hooked up from the dark beneath.

They lay around gulping on the planks
like victims of a gas attack, for whom
no love or remedy was in the offing,
but fried for supper made us into survivors
or hunter-gatherers, part of the main stream;
not adolescents pleased with our exam results,
but exiles from the Rift Valley, moving north
not in a stone boat but an appointed dream.

The Beachcombing

FOR DENNIS O'DRISCOLL

I

Rising early I find the sea in curlers.
Not that it minds, because I'm a non-person,
Hardly someone to keep it from its chores –
Scrubbing the ancient beach, washing the feet
Of the dilapidated cliffs and skerries.

Covenanted to perpetual drudgery
It has no option but to bend its back
And get on with the levelling down,
Dreaming while it works of time off in lieu,
Days when it might catch up with its sleep.

The morning after last week's north-easter,
When the foreshore had turned over a new leaf
And the shells I used to hold to my ear
Had been buried for palaeontology's future,
My eye lit on a fisherman's good-luck charm

Tangled in sea-lettuce and carrageen.
Oxidized metal, given by wife or girlfriend,
Was it Peter, Nicholas, even Andrew?
Whoever's martyrdom had been relied on,
The opposing forces had won that round –

Or so my nature drove me to assume.
Other days someone's dog might prance about,
A heraldic supporter on the loose,

Showering sand and wet over my trousers
While gulls circled above me, taking note.

Debris stuck between high water and low
Caught at my perambulating feet and eyes,
Dead things, things become junk, uncared for, jettisoned,
Plastic bottles asleep under the bladderwrack,
Like babes in the woods around Enniscorthy,

And indestructible tangles, cordage
Strong enough for a hanging, orange and cyan.
All this time my footprints trod on my heels
And the ferry – used to be called the mail-boat–
Slid out from the lee of Killiney Head,

Steering unstoppably for the east,
Tall, impersonal, with its nose in the air –
A coloured cut-out towed from wing to wing –
Incommunicado, hiding its feelings
And all its lachrymose comings and goings.

Did I want to be left behind, with burins
Of resentment engraving my blank features?
But the future could hardly happen without me,
Whatever the drinkers in The Bleeding Horse
Decided about my soft words and havering.

Sixty miles south Charon & Co were ferrying
Other gatherings of uncertain souls

Back and forth in their closed high-sided ships
(Hell's circles no longer being concentric)
As the sun shifted somewhere above the Tuskar.

The stuff around my shoes, cuttle-bone, razor-
Shells, a crab's pale underparts and extremities
Mixed up with strands of dark red algae, slopped
Round and about with the noisy shemozzle
Made by waves stumbling over their own feet,

Left me thinking of souls, like puffs of steam
Floating from the gullets of shrieking peacocks
And carried away downwind to nowhere
(Though the attribution of souls to shellfish
May not have the approval of theocrats).

Today's lot of rubbish is a new chapter –
The jellyfish spread out like cultured colonies
In a Petri dish, bacilli on agar-agar,
Drying in the sun as the desert fathers
Dried at their orisons in the Sahara,

And a washed-up lifebelt, white and scarlet zero,
Knocked about by the waves, the paint rubbed thin,
But the letters DEVON C C just readable,
Like a weak voice calling through atmospherics –
Though the drift of the message passes me by.

The dunlin picking about in the sand rise up
When I overstep an invisible threshold
And swirl in unison in the middle distance,
Turning as one, as an African hand might turn,
Pale palm showing briefly in the sunlight.

Further off, where something shapeless is lying,
Herring gulls are standing around like students
At an anatomy lesson, one or two
Even lending a hand with the post mortem.
Nothing much there, I fancy, for my sack.

II

An overcast day, the cloud-coloured waves
Thudding on my left and the cries of sea-birds
Working on my spirits. But the haul is good,
Namely, a baby's comforter, half a comb
And a canister labelled toxic waste.

The latter must be good for an interview,
A fee and a night's oblivion in Wicklow.
As for the comb it ought to come in handy
For someone with only half a head of hair.
(Staying cheerful can be a full-time job.)

Later I steer clear of bathers a mile off,
People being more dangerous than asps,

Though after-images of the younger females
Float on my retina for hours to come,
Rising and falling with the tidal cycle.

It is said that the girls left in the sea
Are as good as any that came out of it,
Even if the best fish swim near the bottom
And have to be searched for. Though not by me,
For whom drowning is nobody's business.

The hairs on my legs and body are aligned
With the drag of the waters off Mombasa,
Where my ancestors tested the new medium
But found it inimical to the mind.
The sea's my provider, not my element.

Offshore a fishing boat goes round in circles
Searching for its cork floats and marker buoys,
Stewed tea in a pot on the galley stove
And cigarettes between wind-hardened lips
Like pegs stuck any old how in a cribbage-board.

If it's whiting they're after they can keep them —
Fish that God must have designed for the meek
And those repenting what they thought were sins.
But the birds are keen enough, crying out loud
About emptiness and the needy young.

Afternoon, and a snare among the dunes –
An empty wallet, with its false smile uppermost.
I kick it into the tangles of marram grass,
Being one to keep clear of police courts
And the apologetics of petty crime.

A sore thumb on the unlimited strand,
I've never asked to be looked at, never
Aspired to kingship or yearned for plaudits,
Never been one to beat a bronze-bound ball
Up into the sky with a mud-stained hurley.

It is for me to state, you to believe
In the time you buy with your surplus value.
The bluffs are not called that for nothing
And they'll resist the battering of the sea
For long enough to see me out, and you.

Someone approaches, a woman in boots
And mac, walking a weary spayed retriever.
I give her the time of day, but she just narrows
Her eyes, with closed-mouth smile, and marches on,
Anxiousness trailing like a waft of scent.

When I look round I see that she does not.
The clouds stay closed for the sunset, and darkness
Will soon be shooing me into my hut
For beans and bacon and rearranging blankets
And communion with my half comb and comforter.

From a Submariner's Diary

The routine is to surface in the morning,
Checking first that I'm clear of polar ice,
Then struggle out on to the conning tower
For a breath of the unaccomplished future,
While petrels skitter off to the horizon,
Flicking the tops of the feather-edged waves.

Down below, in the sad recycled air,
There have been the usual hare-brained dramas,
Watched with feelings of fear or impassivity.
Bound every night to join in these inanities,
Put together out of a lifetime's rubbish,
I despair of discovering an exit.

Lacking windows, the goings-on outside
Are matters of doctrine and speculation.
Blind men swing axes in a blacked-out room.
Tilting the hydroplanes will bring me up,
But then the periscope, when free of mist,
Shows only heaving sea, driven by wind.

Weather permitting, the watertight hatch
Can be unfastened to restore my spirits.
Recently, standing on the spray-dashed platform,
I sighted land, somewhere like Hispaniola,
An outcrop furred over by forms of life,
Which, if they saw me, saw me as small beer.

The close-packed woods hung round the hills' shoulders
Like Persian lamb, over the tiers of roofs
Drifted what seemed to be domestic smoke
And there were flying brickbats, small-arms fire
And screaming, audible beyond the bar,
Telling me of other ways to go under.

House of Words

Houseflies circle round the electrolier
In a room whose air has been breathed to death,
  Where the windows are covered with words
    And I cannot see out,
More like a cellar than a belvedere.

The hot messages and assertions prod
At my eyes to check that I'm wide awake.
  They press down on me like Roman shields.
    I yearn to wield a spray-can
And make known the unprintable name of God.

When I peel back a noun to glimpse the sky,
With a fingernail overdue for cutting,
  Outside all is astronomers' darkness.
    What might be arms and legs
Are after-images floating in the eye.

Behind the Window

FOR LIZ

Swift as a swift or still as cactus
    Or working hand and eye –
Those, roughly speaking, are the options,
    Some more tiring than others,
For filling the time between sleeps.

I picture you slogging through heather
    In newly dubbined boots;
The hawks have been shot or poisoned,
    As no doubt you'll have heard,
And many red deer are tubercular.

You have picked the strenuous path,
    But I prefer to stare
Past the passion-flower almost blocking
    The daylight from my window.
Electricity burns all day,

My thoughts and words gather slowly
    Like drops of limy water
On the cavern's roof, running down
    The beginnings of stalactites
To deposit a grain of meaning.

The dictionaries on my right
    Are albums of old snapshots,
Pictures of forebears and collaterals
    And cousins of the living, known
Mainly to palaeologists.

Burnt matches can be stuck together
    On rainy days to build
A simulacrum of St Paul's,
    The Taj, the Tower of Babel,
But not to create a new earth.

It's the language of the street cries
    That possesses and galvanizes
What I use instead of a heart –
    Which is known as a mind
And is odourless and invisible.

Mostly my window's double glass
    Keeps these noises without
And myself within; while my wheel-chair
    Baulks at the front stone steps –
A horse with a sixth sense for danger.

Sometimes there's a knock at the door
    And I trundle my chair
Along the lino in the hall
    To turn the mortise-lock.
Enters a stranger with new phrases,

Infecting me like blankets shipped
    From a world plagued by love.
But the fever burns itself out
    Before the sun goes down
And once again I fail to qualify

For pain-killing pills (the white pills!)
   Or a nurse with cool hands.
Getting myself to bed takes time,
   With the need for clean dressings
And callipers to be unstrapped.

When the hours for sleeping come round
   The street's sodium lamps
Cast hot brown light over my ceiling
   And there's somebody dribbling
A cola can along the pavement.

The next day's words will not lie down,
   They circle like mosquitoes
Not quite able to make their minds up
   But dying to be heard.
Eventually dreams roll in

And there you are, trudging the mountains,
   Thinking less about nature
Than about the grit in your boots
   And the aches that will be soothed
By your companion of the night.

Daffodils

Might as well have a guard dog as these foghorns
Of daffodils on parade outside the house.
I made my dates and travelled by clockwork train,
Trusting the caretakers, Héloïse, my mouse,
And the wolf-spider with sensitive feet.

I had my office hours in the garden shed,
Hidden among stakes and bundles of bamboo,
Where wasps had colonized an empty box,
Pandora's possibly, and hearing what I knew
Were ambulances whooping down the street.

An Evening In

Cold, they cried, as I turned towards the fire,
Cold, colder, North Pole!, as I ran my eyes
Over the bits and pieces on the mantelshelf
Before changing course, heading for the sideboard,
The candlesticks, decanters and coloured ware.

I pointed my finger at a Dog of Fo,
Warmer, a voice said from the sofa, warmer;
Then when I moved across to touch your hair
I was hot, they chorused, hot, hotter, burning.
You were the thing they'd chosen as decoy.

So you saw me angry. Shy too. The tricks
One puts up with, grinning like a Jolly Roger!
Can you forgive me for being a boy?
Tomorrow, when the hyenas have left us
And the paraffined kindling spits and cracks

And the coals glow neon in the dark,
When your parents have vanished away
And our bread's been buttered, let me relax
On your soft angora-covered shoulder
And make French toast with my yard-long toasting-fork.

Tennis in Wicklow

I knew from the way you spooned the ball
Back to me over the sagging net,
Reaching out awkwardly with your racket
And little cries of mock despair,
That you were not an opponent I could live with.

Your sister watched us from the conservatory,
Smoothing down her fringe and throwing words
To a recent victim of her backhand,
Whose short back and sides were just visible
Among the pelargoniums and nerines.

Television

The handsome man kisses the beautiful woman
The beautiful woman's mouth remains ajar
The laughing girl at the steering wheel looks sideways
At the inadequate boy who is hallucinating
At the window of an oceanside apartment
At sunset on the evening of the sixth day

The mouth that is ajar appears to be moist
The landscape beyond the steering wheel is desert
The hallucinations have to do with fish
In undersea follies that were built by divers
In the last days of an omnipotent somebody
In memory of his much loved wife and mother

The apartment's windows are alive with lightning
The desert has been requisitioned by soldiers
The fish bide their time before storming the gates
Of the laughing girl with firearms and expressions
Of desire on their unsmiling physiognomies
Of which the underhung jaws are made a feature

The handsome man clearly has the gift of words
The inadequate boy fails to attract sympathy
The steering wheel must have a life of its own
To make sense of the pile-up on the freeway
To labourers like ourselves, home from the rice-fields
To scrape the barrel for our adequate children

The sounds do not divide themselves into words
The words that can be guessed at are without meaning
The shadows of meaning are cast by psychoses
But the inadequate boy has food and drink
But the laughing girl flashes her perfect teeth
But the beautiful woman oozes contentment

The unemployed are sitting under the bo-tree
The headman's television has them in trance
The gold watch of the hypnotist is outmoded
For the dolce vita can be seen laid out
For light-gathering eyes and appetites ready
For stimulation as if by Spanish fly

The laughing girl circles the earth in a space suit
The beautiful woman's orange groves are fruiting
The handsome man has an artificial heart
His peasant's complexion speaks of a good guy
His sperm no longer have the will to swim
His machines for killing are the ne plus ultra

The Sharp End

Our cadre is sharp as the north wind,
as ignorant as an oil refinery,
    as brute as fact.

When the Word was revealed to the Secretary
we were enlisted for the long haul,
    the crowning act.

The destruction of comforts came first,
then the proclamation that security
    did not exist.

When this had been established, expulsions
followed as night follows night. We chose
    names from a list.

Who requires a Professor of Culture?
Or a guardian of ancestors' graves
    over the hill?

Let them learn to be miners of pitchblende
or to collect carcasses and nightsoil
    if they are ill.

The old are not easy on the eyes;
weak, too, and when shouted at directly,
    likely to weep.

On the march their faces run with tears,
which does nothing to improve our tempers
    and spoils our sleep.

That they should dig their own graves is tempting –
with time for the last rites, and then exit
    without delay –

but nurturing such a dream is weakness.
Milestones must be passed and norms exceeded
    every day.

It's forbidden to avert the eyes
from the solar flare that is illuminating
    our mildewed land.

Even a worker with worthy goals
can trip and fall on these slimy steps,
    this barren strand.

As for the riff-raff with soft fingers,
they shall crumble statues with a sledge,
    their backs shall break

and their memories shall be wiped clean.
There shall be no irony, no mistresses
    and no mistake.

In our citadel we sing in unison,
our songs dispersing the swarms of error
        that blind our youth

and recalling for the prudent citizen
doctrines that re-educated sages
        endorse as truth.

Post-Glacial

When the glaciers' frost-bitten toes dropped off
And the U-shaped valleys filled with sea
Birch and pine came out of their hiding-places,

Survival was no longer everything, brain
Had time to think about its dissolution
And about the need for a quid pro quo.

As the sun had finally turned up trumps,
He might expect more than the old-fashioned
Puff oblique. They could not define worship,

But something on those lines seemed to be called for,
Something extreme, going against their grain,
Gifts to ward off another death of food.

While the south wind ran round behind the bushes
And blew upon their organizing wits
Legends constructed themselves like rumours,

Truth being what the elders said was truth.
There was no denying the days got longer
And warmer after those awful ceremonies.

Not everyone understood the new codes,
But infringements never went unpunished.
Loose women were always made an example of.

These glimpses through the wrong end of a telescope
Make me wonder who is observing whom.
In case the arrow of time flies both ways

I tighten the girdle of my wide-sleeved gown
And take up my position on the mat,
Ready to learn the art of the soft fall.

The Glutton

A solo glutton or wolverine
Shambles through the woods like an automaton,
Facial hair caked with the blood of caribou.
It's all snow and howling wind and hunger.

His race is on the way to extinction,
But just in time a wildlife photographer
Will track his footprints among the hemlocks
And capture his starving backlit eyes.

There are human settlers in the valley.
The heat is turned up high in their cabins
Where a trapper drunkenly inseminates
His unwilling wife against a sink.

Glenasmole

'Glenasmole' translates as 'valley of the thrushes'.
I too would hear them calling out to the world,
Making their declarations from the larches
Beside the lake at either end of the day,
Each stanza reprised to drive the message home.

Those threats and enticements were nobody's business
But the thrushes', music only to romantics
Taken up as always with death and self,
Lighthouse winking to lighthouse along the coast.

Thrush soup was once esteemed in Heligoland –
Thirty or forty to the pot were recommended
By Herr Grätke, the famous ornithologist.
The autumn migration then was a phenomenon.

And those celebrated Italian recipes
For thrush paté with dashes of Marsala
Are edited out of the cookery programmes
Broadcast from Milan before the children's bedtime.

Hereabouts the smell is of mouldy hay,
Reminding us of phosphorus and its works.
Let us go out then and practise being penitent
In the silent pigeon-populated fields.

Glenasmole now has its solitaries, flitting
Between the alders, senses tuned to receive

Warnings and conjurations that rarely come—
Lonely, if that's how you see them, or defenders
Of the last bridgehead, as they themselves might put it.

Sestina for the European Eel

Ever since genesis the forms of rain
Have flowed like godsends off maternal hills
To quench the thirst of their unthirsty children,
Those who light-heartedly abandon ship
And shimmy round in the Sargasso harbour
Where anchorage is toasted in its absence.

There squid are known by presence more than absence,
Eager to strike, like buzzards after rain,
Below the floating tangleweeds that harbour
Kindergartens ignorant of the hills
Whose freshets mobilized the mother-ship
And underwrote what were to be her children.

Not that the larvae see themselves as children.
Sargassum hides them in their parents' absence,
Fronds wave farewell to the receding ship
And stir their salt into the callow rain.
The tales that circulate are tales of hills
And waterfalls and sad adieus in harbour.

So play-days end with exodus from harbour,
The grand collective movement of the children
Back over years to legendary hills,
Rivers whose thoughts meander in the absence
Of regimens that get to grips with rain
And havens deep enough to float a ship.

The current takes them, slower than a ship
But faster than a sea-snail to their harbour.
Those who win through are out of tune with rain
That weeps on water for the preyed-on children,
Never remembered, even for their absence,
By those in rivers round the feet of hills.

Under the turned-up collars of the hills
Elvers slide through the shadow of a ship,
Saluting with a fondness born of absence
What might have been a visionary harbour
And feeding for the future of their children
In winding waterways spotted by rain.

Feeling in their bones the absence of children,
Bound by hills that are curtained off by rain,
Each runs from harbour like a smugglers' ship.

The Lifeboat

We woke this morning in Fanning's Hotel
Tangled up like leftovers of spaghetti
And disengaged ourselves into awareness
Of the harbour's seagulls rattling their sabres,
Eyes peeled, each low ga-ga-gah a reminder
    Of who is master there.

Perhaps the union of souls is a will-o'-the-wisp
And less attractive than I thought last night.
Herring-gulls of thirty are not unknown,
Which says something for the embattled state.
Some die younger, but not of broken hearts
    Or yearning or despair.

Last week, just after closing time, the lifeboat
Was called out to some ferry in distress.
The crew lumbered along in waterproof gear,
The doors flew open, each station was manned
And the dark blue hull shot down, cradle screaming
    On the corroded track.

Seagulls, of course, are home-birds after dark,
Switched off on their ledges; but down below
The boat heaved out of sight in clouds of spray
Just beyond the pier-heads. Crossing our fingers
We conjured up the freezing scud and rated
    Gull white against man black.

East Cliff, West Bay

Tired of Devonian and Carboniferous,
I am smitten by this Jurassic wall
Which parades itself on a bench of limestone
Nibbled at by waves that never give up.

Would you say it was a mile high? Well, hardly,
But about half a football pitch on end
With seagulls overhead gives you the feel of it,
Honey-coloured, too, or precisely ochre.

The ghost of an Indian temple pushes
Its way through the eroded sandy face,
With travesties of mullions, mouldings, ribs,
String courses, lintels, astragals and lockbands,

Panels of censored sculpture, hoodmoulds, balusters,
Corbels, stalks and beads, blunted by a wind
Blowing since before the crash of the dinosaurs.
Au fond are sprag-sided doors into darkness.

Up above, the fulmar run a tight ship.
They cuddle into cavities, take note
Of sashaying devils on two legs and four,
And make their sorties for Heaven knows what.

Stones scattered over the buff-coloured beach
In the shape of buns, baps, muffins and polypores
Are a foretaste of Chesil; and reflected
Waves that collide with the incoming breakers

Fling out emergency spray, as a threatened
Juggler, faced by a rabble of Pekinese,
Might throw up his two handfuls of white balls
Before going down for the last time.

Inshore

I opened a porthole on the weather-side
And found myself looking out on expectations,
A sea so boring something just had to happen.
If you trusted the maps, France was over there,
But what about all the in-between, the waste
    Of waves, the wishy washy space?
    Sometimes an ocean-going smudge
Moved slowly along the join of sky and Channel,
    But failed to make my pulses race.

The outlook shifted from blue to grey to slate
And there was drizzle from one to two-fifteen.
Well, hot-diggity, as they said in the westerns,
Where are all the wonders – flukes and dorsal fins,
Icarus, the Kraken, even submarines
    That can heave themselves up like whales,
    Raw water sluicing off their flanks?
Yes, yes, I can see the chaps in little boats
    Killing time with their shrouds and sails.

Your porthole was to starboard, facing north
And a view of cliffs larded with dragons' teeth,
Which somehow didn't germinate. This you told me
On the intercom in your husky contralto,
With adverse comments on the masculine torsos
    That stepped across your line of sight
    With their medicine balls and surfboards
And that brightly coloured clobber, gearing up
    For whatever they do at night.

That was your line. But did you invent the ambulance
That swooped in with its siren diminuendo
To halt by the ice-cream kiosk, paramedics
At the double down to the surf, where amateur
Revivalists were thumping and blowing, watched
   By the curiously concerned?
   Hearing a tremor in the vowels
I sense one who, looking in a mirror, pictures
   Cockle-shells launched and towers burned.

Odours of the galley drift through our locked cabins
(Mine giving on to colour field and chimera,
Yours opposite the visitors' mini-market),
Though ship's biscuit is all we're likely to get.
Like you I insist on reading while I eat,
   Weighing the pages down with knives
   (Perhaps you've learned to do the same?) –
So many books to be got through, lives of lovers,
   Stories of other people's wives.

To the South and Back

The highway, as the word suggests,
Took us up to the mountain pass
And what is called its bracing air,
Rather than through ravines and tunnels,
Dank, draughty and policed by cold fish.
The views from the col were spectacular
(And we remarked on the tautology),
But we could not discern the elephants
Noted by an earlier traveller
Or swallow all those red and black
Frankly alarmist warning notices
Decorated with skulls and zigzags
About the risk of death from lightning.

Dabbing fitfully at the brakes
We made a serpentine descent
To the plain where the local tongue
Was all inseparable phonemes
And sign language became our lifeline.
Naturally there were signs for silence –
A finger laid across the lips
(With the usual overacting)
Or someone-or-other's listless limbs
Dangled over the edge of a hammock –
But sleep was always hard to come by.

The fact that our pink-and-white reticence
Had nothing at all to do with tongue-tie
We found tricky to put across
By pantomime or tick-tack, given
The scepticism of the natives,
Even when well disposed or loving.
Though ebullience has its charms,
There is much to be said for phlegm.
(A touch of envy here? Perhaps.)

Then, determined to have its say,
The masonry showed us inscriptions
In what seemed to be Roman characters,
But we never got past the dates.
A gecko darted across a pitted
Block, and went to earth below
What may have been an oleander.

We returned by the marble hills
Where in the workings of a quarry
You found an aluminium spoon,
Which is now at rest in our kitchen
Among rolling-pins and carvers.

We used to study its stem,
Arguing and trying to decipher
That half-obliterated trademark –

'Union', 'Torino' or 'Inox'.

In Puerto Montt

Just off this earthquake coast the sea-urchins are infested
with underwater spiders, said to be poisonous.
Selling the urchins on the quayside, fishermen
crack open the shells, and cautious buyers watch
for the eight-legged parasites scurrying off
to hide under hawsers and bits of bladderwrack.
No doubt they feature in jokes among the locals,
but the Chilean patois is beyond me –
and behind the laughter behind my back.

My rubber boots slither on scales and fishskin.
The smell of ammonia kills most kinds of appetite
and belly-down in what looks like Humboldt's bilge
a small penguin scavenges in the harbour.
Nose pink, eyes complaining about the wind,
I see you advance from the cleaning shed
between pine-trees with snow tangled in their needles.
You look so crotchety I wonder if a spider
will have to be freed from that designing head.

Eldorado

In the valley the noise was the noise of insects,
Little machines locked in a struggle for power
With no remission given for good behaviour,
But up here on the slated roof of the world
It's the wind that takes over the vacant airspace,
Doubling for the voices of unemployed gods.

Pot-hatted and squatting behind the bus shelter,
Multiple-skirted women are smoking pipes
And hawking said-to-be ancient figurines
To tourists uneasy about them and us.
But when Anne has snagged her 15-denier tights
On a much buffeted fender we all relax.

The air rushes past, whisking away its oxygen
To those more barrel-chested than myself.
This is a place where history has been sucked
Into caverns cut off by underground water,
Where even the best diver's breath gives out
Before the roof lifts its dripping head in darkness.

There's little but dry grass and shale, pushed up
For hungering birds to scavenge on, and peasants
Genuflecting to someone's imported deity.
But back at the Gran Hotel and the world of credit
A trio that knows all about syncopation
Is beguiling the dance-floor with father's favourites.

The sanitized saxophone emits its sorrow
And Anne moves gracefully amongst her peers –
Several gold-bearing strata being exposed,
Ripe for delivery to the crushing mills,
From whose indigenous gangers and charge-hands
Words of understanding will not be looked for.

Pangolins

In grandfather's day, when my unattached soul
Was still waiting off-stage in a cowrie shell,
The ritualized consumption of pangolins
Was a highlight of the elders' working week,
Scheduled for the hush between the evening thunder
And bedtime, when the hyraxes started up,
Howling like demons until two in the morning.
Dancers in nightmarish masks were under contract
To shuffle about on stilts, while the élite
Exchanged pleasantries and got on with the eating.
Their ceremonial spoons of imported brass,
Greened over with carbonate and a film of fat,
Are now collectors' items, much in demand,
Disciplined and demystified under glass.

Intended to mollify a group of spirits
Whose ill will might otherwise bring down afflictions,
The observances were festal on the surface,
The younger contingent danced, and a good time
Was had by everyone except the pangolins.
However, a darker underside emerged
In the effigies of those to be placated
Sheltering under the eaves of the cult house.
Their names escape me now, but the slot-like mouths
And hungry chins of their reliquary figures
Looked short on sympathy, and hotly incarnate
Female deities overpowered their slaves
With those heavy breasts, traditionally scarified,
That jut out downwards and sideways to our graves.

No doubt the oblique set of the bulging eyes
And the dark patina of uncertain origin
Gave these entities quite a *je ne sais quoi*,
Enhanced by awareness of their private parts,
Among them anal orifices burned deep
For the insertion of a magical paste. –
No, it's not how we do things now, but the track
Down to the lake in the impact crater twists,
The water trembles like lead in a plumber's ladle
And nature mauls us, just as she did our ancients.
The warrior ants keep on asserting their right
To almost everything under the crown
And the pangolin writhes at the heart of the mystery
Back there in the hinterland of our history.

The Gaffer's Tale

We left by the Elephant Gate,
not forgetting to pass small coins
to the minions and hangers-on
who loitered around the watch-house.
The bearers, of course, had been sent ahead
to uncover possible ambushes,
inactivate tripwires
and spring the mantraps.
When we reached it, the bamboo forest
was just as bad as we'd feared;
even our second-sighted guide
could barely recognize the track
or its overgrown remains.
It was long grass in all directions,
over our heads and bumps of location
(hence the expression 'bamboozled').

En route, we thought, for the lost city,
it was the sight of the white rhino
that overturned the apple-cart.
Purveying phoney aphrodisiacs
to chinless wonders east of Suez
was not why we were braving
the war of the louse.
Rumours of ruins in the hill tracts,
with sculpted gods in twos and threesomes
coupling in high relief –
that was what drew us on,
loaded down with temperamental cameras,

satellite dishes and prophylactics.
The public wishes to be informed.
Anyway our party got through unscathed,
The crossfire passing over our heads –

no thanks, though, to the Presidential Guard,
a four-man detachment of whom
was foisted on us for protection
during the haggling in the capital.
But for our shikarees (as they call them
in a country I shall not name)
we should have joined the rhinoceroses
as food for kites and vultures.
With their loved but obsolete weapons
they saved our yellowing skins
and did something for their own kudos,
though in the last exchange
a stray round glancing off a boulder
transformed a member of the Guard
from one of the indolent élite
into a fallen animal.

Once we were into teak country
the sailing was plain, the hazards fewer.
The loggers had ruined the north,
but down south it was easy walking
through motionless stands of timber,
where high-up invisible bell-birds

made noises best described as plangent,
as though testing a hall's acoustics.
It was far from the fields of poppies
and the routes of the traffickers
with armed baddies in dusty pick-ups.
In one clearing we shot some footage
of a colony of golden monkeys
being all too anthropomorphic,
thinking this would appeal to the networks
and concerned viewers worldwide.

Then it was secondary scrub
and clambering over sills of trap
all the way up to the bluff,
beyond which we got into sand
and what was called the 'no-go desert'.
Our tents were proof against mosquitoes,
though Knong Nut declared she was bitten
through the nylon. This was no place
for a pea princess, pretty or not.
Director's Assistant, how are you!
I'm the first to admit her looks
steered my thoughts in one sweet direction,
but, as looks so often do, they lied —
or the signs had me out of my depth.
So we struck out across the grit
for the hills we couldn't spell.

And there they were, in full chiaroscuro
on the sunlit grain of sandstone,
gymnastic lovers at their exercises.
Complicities had been sworn to,
movements settled in rehearsal
and this was the enactment.
A leg around his waist, she smiled
with barely parted lips, a private smile
to a world behind the scenes.
Off-stage, before another audience,
mortars were targeting the village
where Knong Nut's parents had their childhood.
She seemed unmoved, possibly thinking
of the night ahead and its fallout,
the rules for the good life
and those fireflies, if that's what they were.

Chloe

You are welcome to stay until four,
But we find it can perturb the residents
If strangers are present during tea.

The young lady you have come to visit –
Chloe to you, but we call her Kerry –
Is in the day-room, next to the toilets.

You can see her there, in the white trainers
And slightly oversize maroon track suit,
Beached on the vinyl-covered settee.

We are reviewing her medication.
She looks stable, but should there be problems
Please ring for the Senior Care Assistant.

Yes, she rocks her body to and fro,
Like that, strongly from morning to night.
Sometimes she buzzes into her hand.

But don't let any of this concern you.
It is typical of the disorder
And one might say without being heartless

That it gives her a purpose in life
As well as some desirable exercise.
And it keeps the pneumonia at bay.

Twenty-two, she has never said a word,
And what she sees through her flax-blue eyes
Is known to no one. If without warning

She should put your arm around her shoulders
And bury her head in your woolly breast,
Remember that it signifies nothing;

She will shortly resume her rocking
And what another visitor called
Piling sandbags on the levee.

But she eats well and – it's obvious –
The profession is able to banish
All the visible symptoms of suffering.

A Family Man

FOR MARY

The dreams of Westerners are set in concrete,
But I, as a nomad, dream about the steppes
And the dry valleys that, if followed for weeks,
Ultimately take you down into the ricelands,
Which I have never seen (or want to see).

Riding over the plain on my little horse
The clouds being hurried across the blue remind me
That I am no more than a flag of convenience
Under which my sons can sail into the future
(Daughters, too, but that I must keep to myself).

Portrait of a Woman from the Fayum

The painter of mummy portraits came today
And spoke to father about my symptoms.
Overhearing words like 'mortal illness',
I was not surprised, given how I feel.
A girl, they call me, but I look years older,
My skin the colour of papyrus, brown eyes
Facing other eyes with open-ended questions
And a mind that gloats over the present,
Having no wish to be other-worldly.

When he comes to make a sketch from the life,
With his paints, brushes, charcoal stove and wax,
I shall put on my emeralds and garnets,
Small though they are, as well as my gold ball earrings,
With an understated Roman-style fringe
Above my forehead and enquiring eyebrows.
And I shall ask my mother to dress my body
In that fine peplum (with the purple border),
When the real me has embarked for the underworld.

I've not been specially good, but I've tried
Not to scandalize the impartial gods.
Forgive me, self-pity is wrong, I know,
But tears seem to have a will of their own.
Through the doorway I can see the bulrushes
Swaying in the wind off the Libyan desert
And hear the teal burbling on Lake Moeris,
While down the road the light-hearted village women
Ululate at someone else's wedding feast.

Icarus

After the falling apart
We pulled on protective clothing
And hunted through steaming wreckage,
Desperate to find the brain-box.
But a pearl-diver located it
Among gastropods and corals.

Plugging it into the monitor,
There were signals, sure enough,
Some bizarre patterns of waves
And an occasional cry
As of one soon to be defeated
But not to be understood.

Easy to predict the headlines,
The allocation of blame
And the laying-out of flowers.
That Daedalus got to Sicily
Left him wide open to charges
Of using inferior wax.

Mismatch

So many windows to the right and left
(Windows for gazing out from, not peering in through),
And the shallow steps, treads worn in the middle,
Leading me up to a gorilla's door,
The architrave so high, the knocker monstrous:

It swings away from me and there you are,
Fair hair, just as I remember, and the smile —
But all that *darkness* above you, the *space*,
The candelabrum, cirrus of cigar smoke
And self-collected laughter in the distance!

Those landowners in their gilt frames are dead
A century or more, but you're their property;
And this mad double-dealing staircase, when
And to what occasions did it advance things?
Why did you keep all this under your hat?

I want to skedaddle, sleep in the ha-ha,
Rerun my past in tandem with your future —
No, we can never keep in step, your pace
Will always be streets ahead of my flat feet.
I should be lumped in with your father's pheasants,

And halfway through a shoot he'd grin to recognize
My limp corpse deposited at his feet,
A drop of blood lingering in my nostril,
As the beaters advanced like robots
And the guns banged and echoed in the combe.

My allotment is in a different theatre –
The craft pottery at the end of the lane,
Where I think revolutionary thoughts
And the outcome, slippery from my fingers,
Is fired up (when I can afford the fuel).

Always, to start with, clay tried to escape me;
Thrown and gathered, squeezed and pressed down into,
It squirmed, reared up or slithered out sideways,
Proteus running wild in my earthy cell.
But I defeated him with my non-violence –

A contemplative form of unarmed combat.
Before long I had him bound under glazes,
Meekly holding my scented orange pekoe
While visitors assessed his epigones,
Though they rarely carried anything off.

It was chance or a convergence of lifelines
That the two of us shared a spliff in The Star
(You with a bellyache about your family),
Since when we have never looked round or back –
Till today and the appearance of seigneury.

*

Now I know your secrets and you know mine
The voyage home will not be on a spice ship.
In the trades the manatees will be silent

As the grey crests go sliding past our flanks
And we run before the wind for the roadstead,

Stealing at dawn into the tidal basin,
Where we tie up just astern of the dredger
And the patrol boats of Customs and Excise.
You can motor away over the hill
While I make my way up Market Jew Street,

Thinking of the stone in St Mary's churchyard
To the memory of Henry M. Fudge,
Departed this life eighteen twenty-two,
Aged two years and five months, before he had
Time to unpack and play with his illusions.

Air Show

The grand flying display has finished,
Small boys have pondered the cockpits
Of obsolete fighters and peered
Through long since declassified bomb-sights,
And parachutists, small and frail,
Have descended on spiders' filaments
To crumple near the canvas target.
As a finale flying sharks
Browbeat everyone with their engines
And voided multicoloured smokes
All over the spectators' sky.

Across the fifty-acre car park
Small parties are loading their hatchbacks,
Calling to friends and slamming doors
Before setting off for their futures.
I watch the field empty like an hour-glass.
In remote hangars still warm aircraft
Are being fondled by their mechanics,
But the birds have called it a day.
One crow passes on its way to somewhere,
A planet and assorted stars
Clock in, but do not leave a message.

Eve's Lament
KUNO MEYER'S 1911 TRANSLATION IN 'ANCIENT IRISH POETRY'

The poem hangs low in the sky,
Worn out and crusted, but the glow
From its radioactive innards
Still lights up today's dark matter.

Fancy Dress

Everyone in these parts is in disguise.
Some have the protective colourings of accountants,
Others of students, housewives and sexpots.
In our village many are disguised as widows.

The domino is more or less obligatory.
One person tried to get by without disguise
And found himself sent down for life.

Camouflaged as a writer of poems,
I cannot stop fiddling with my necklace.